BACKSTAGE WITH GOD

RECONCILING SCIENCE TO THE GENESIS CREATION
FROM A CHRIST CENTERED POINT OF VIEW

GENE MAXWELL

Copyright © 2022 by Gene Maxwell. All rights reserved.

All rights reserved. No part of this book may be reproduced or transmitted in any form or by any means, electronic or mechanical, including photocopying, recording, or by any information storage and retrieval system without express written permission from the author, except in the case of brief quotations embodied in critical reviews and certain other noncommercial uses permitted by copyright law.

Published in the United States of America

Brilliant Books Literary
137 Forest Park Lane Thomasville
North Carolina 27360 USA

CHAPTERS

Chapter 1   A Journey 9

Chapter 2   A Creator 14

Chapter 3   A Priori 18

Chapter 4   A Beginning 24

Chapter 5   A Choice 29

Chapter 6   A Matter of Matter 37

Chapter 7   An Explanation 41

Chapter 8   A Moment or Two 50

Chapter 9   A Different Frame of Reference 58

Chapter 10   A Comparison 67

Bibliography 75

References 77

Scripture quotations, unless otherwise indicated, are taken from the New King James version Bible published by Thomas Nelson.

A PROLOGUE

I undertook the writing of Backstage with God with the express purpose of giving glory to God through a better understanding of His word and a revelation of what science says about His creation. I fully subscribe to God's word as being inspired by Him and infallibly communicated in the original letters as they were written. I also believe that modern translations, for the most part, accurately represent the meanings of these original letters.

However, it is unfortunate that misunderstandings have occurred over the years since the original letters were given to humanity. By misunderstandings, I mean that the Bible, God's word, has been used by some to disallow science, particularly regarding the six days of Genesis. I believe God created the world we live in and humanity in the literal six, twenty-four-hour days as it was written in Genesis. The part I question is, who's clock was being used to measure those days, those hours? It probably wasn't the clock we used today, for the planet did not exist during many of those days.

Christianity has always struggled with a desire to put God in a box to determine how He does what He does when His word isn't always that. An excellent example of that is the six days of creation. Without the details, how are we to know exactly how God achieved creating the universe, earth, and humanity. Perhaps at the time Genesis was written, it was not the right time in the history of man that he should know that. Perhaps God knew that it would be revealed later when people could understand how the universe came about through a scientific explanation of what He did. I believe God reveals Himself, wisdom, and knowledge when a man is ready to receive it. The exception to that would be prophecy as written in His word and in particular with regard to the end times.

Early in the last century, Albert Einstein proposed in his theory of relativity that time is relative, that is, not the same everywhere in the universe. Later, that time depends on velocity, close locations, and gravity. And since God resides outside the universe He created, where time does not exist, He did not require a clock. Time was a construct He used possibly to help humanity measure his days and the seasons of life and communicate the days of creation. But according to Einstein's discovery of the relativity of time, it was a different clock than we use today to tell time. In this book, I will go through a process to establish how the clock of Genesis relates to today's earth clock, as there is a relationship that can be measured.

Furthermore, I believe the truth and value of God's word are not diminished in any way but somewhat enhanced by a better understanding and the clarification that science can bring to this conundrum of how the six days of Genesis were measured and should be understood. Because of a lack of understanding, people have attributed a meaning to the six days of Genesis that, I believe, was never meant to be, nor should God's word have ever discouraged anyone from considering the findings of science. I see no disagreement between the book of Genesis and the main line of scientific discovery, including the Big Bang, which started it all, evolution, and the scientific explanation of how life on earth came into being. I believe it could not have happened without God and the impetus He provided to begin and bring about the whole process as He saw fit.

Even today, we as learners need to be careful that we don't put God into that box based on our understanding, mainly when His word isn't that specific. For example, in Genesis, concerning the creation of man, the Bible says that God formed man out of the dust of the ground and that He created them male and female, which is all the detail we are given. God formed a man from the dust of the land, both male and female. But the question then is, how did he do that? We can imagine all sorts of ways that He could have accomplished what he did, and I submit that science provides a reasonable answer and one that gives more glory to God than leaving it that He somehow just did it. One of the primary purposes for which I wrote this book was to reconcile the findings of science to a better understanding of the six days occurring in the book of Genesis. That is how I will lead my readers throughout this book, giving God glory through science. There is so much that we don't know about God, yet as we study the human body and how it came about, we can begin to see just how amazing our God is. Just as He programmed all the wisdom and knowledge into a tiny bit of energy which ultimately brought about the unfolding of millions of galaxies, stars, and planets, it may also be possible that He programmed all the wisdom and knowledge into the first life on earth that ultimately brought about each of His creatures including man, from the dust of the earth which came to this planet from the many stars God created in the heavens.

In writing this book, I have read many science books from which I have gained the knowledge and information necessary to bring the Bible and science together in the first three chapters of Genesis. Additionally, while writing Backstage with God, I came across an exciting movie which has used a lot of the same information I garnered from the same science books to produce a great and entertaining film with the same goal of reconciling science to the Bible. I recommend you watch The Genesis Code, which will lay a lot of groundwork to help you better understand Backstage with God. I have even used some illustrations from the movie because I thought they would assist readers if they couldn't watch the film. I have read many science books, as well as the cinema

Genesis Code. My writings had only one primary purpose, and that was to bring information to those who were struggling with believing the Bible in light of scientific teachings which disallowed both God and the Bible and to hopefully reduce the misunderstandings about the six days of Genesis.

CHAPTER I

A Journey

My journey began long ago. Growing up I was exposed to God, the Bible, and a form of religion by my maternal grandparents. At a young age my grandmother made sure I was able to name all sixty-six books of the Bible. As I grew, additional information was fed into my mind, but as I remember, most of that information was at a child's level. God made the earth, moon, and sun, but there was nothing about how that was done. He was good and loved everyone, although I was never sure why. As I developed into my teen years and beyond, my intellect grew but knowledge of God remained pretty much the same. I still retained that early understanding of God but the older I got the less relevant He became to my pleasure-seeking life. After graduating high school, I left the little faith I had and began a life seeking pleasure rather than intellectual study as some of my friends did. But God had other plans for my life and at age thirty I first heard the Good News spoken, that Jesus died for my sins. That morning I started a new life and began seeking knowledge about God. It was at this point that I began to apply myself to both my spiritual growth and my intellectual growth. I started taking seminary extension courses from my pastor, Dr. J. Patrick Maloney, who exposed me to studies about God that were intellectual but also very down to earth. I also enrolled in Boyce Bible School for pastors and teachers, which two of my pastors (David White and Dr. J. Patrick Maloney) greatly encouraged. In addition, I began taking college-level courses at community colleges and universities. I was interested in many different subjects, so when I found something, I was interested in, I would enroll and complete that course. However, even though I now have over 200 credit hours, I was never interested in completing a degree program to better myself financially. I was much more interested in acquiring knowledge about specific areas, so I took courses in psychology, sociology, business, electronics, and mathematics.

More recently, at age sixty-nine, I enrolled in the online division of the Art Institute of Pittsburgh and spent the better part of five years studying hotel and restaurant management, earning 110 college credits before quitting with a 4.0 GPA because the remaining classes required for the degree were uninteresting electives. However, through my daily school assignments during those five years, I learned how to use the Internet for research and write three to four papers per week.

I believe during these fifty-some years God was preparing me for the work I am now engaged in: writing about the reconciliation of science and the God of the Bible with regard to the creation in Genesis. But why would God be interested in me writing a book on this topic?

Many have left their childhood faith because it never matured along with their growing intellect. Therefore, as they grew, their faith became less relevant to their adult life, and through their schooling, they were encouraged to seek more meaningful answers to life. I understand that need because I have had to face that same dilemma in my own walk of faith. I too had questions that the immature faith and understanding I grew up with could not answer. However, I was never faced with the dilemma that today's students are faced with. In public schools, many students often learn to not trust their religious beliefs or faith in God, but rather to put their faith in the physical world and the physical sciences that seem to more adequately answer their questions about the universe and how life came about. In early 2017, my direction of study changed radically, and rather than apply myself to knowing the presence of God, I began to explore the earliest history of our universe through modern science. This new search was inspired by a sermon by my pastor early in the year about the Sovereignty of God and the free will of man, a difficult topic to reconcile and understand. I began searching the Internet on that topic and stumbled upon a plethora of information I had not previously encountered. I read pages and pages of lectures and articles, and many books by intellectually mature Christian apologists, Jewish sages of the kabala from a thousand years ago, brilliant physicists (some with atheistic beliefs), MIT graduates, cosmologists, paleontologists, biologists, astronomers, and other people with great common sense who had spent their whole lives studying their discipline. I studied topics ranging from God before the creation, including His foreknowledge, predestination, and justification; how He programmed free will into humankind; His oneness according to the Torah; Einstein's theory and how it changed our concept of time; and of course, an important topic in this book, time dilation, which explains how there is complete agreement between the six days of Genesis and the billions of years science says it has been since the big bang.

For the last forty years I have applied myself to the study of God and His relevance to my life and while it has, at times, been a circuitous route, I have arrived where I am now ready to share my knowledge with others who may be seeking knowledge or who are in need of encouragement in their faith. I am hopeful that this writing encourages those who have lost or outgrown their religious faith to renew their personal faith in the real God who is so much bigger than we can possibly imagine, a God who wants to engage and partner with us in fixing this world, healing relationships and solving problems that have existed since the creation.

In this book we will
- Explore some things that must have been in God's heart before creation,
- Explain the science of the Big Bang (i.e., how God got all of this started), and
- Reconcile modern science to God's perspective, the Biblical six days of creation in Genesis 1.

The title

Backstage with God came to me one morning in a whisper as I was pondering the duality of the universe; specifically, that it consists of what we see as matter, yet theoretical physicists also say it consists of waves, similar to information. And, while we live in a world our senses tell us is very physical, if we step behind the curtain of the stage we live on, we find that this same world is more ethereal, more an intelligent thought than physical. I know that may sound strange, but that is exactly where science is going and has been for some time.[1]

Every writer should have an idea of who their audience is. Who is the book written for, who might be interested in reading the book? Without a focal point the writer has little idea what should be included or not. It's like aiming an arrow at nothing and shooting it just to see where it goes. So, that being said, the following information in this introduction has been included to 1) provide some background information, and 2) help both this writer and his readers know what we're aiming at.

Before I began the actual writing of *Backstage with God*, I watched Andy Stanley deliver a message titled "Who Needs God" via a videotape at our church. The following excerpt was part of that sermon by Andy Stanley, who is the senior pastor of North Point Community Church, Alpharetta, Georgia:

For some, the question is "Do we need God?" For others, the question is "do we need religion?" More Americans are giving up or backing away from religion. It's not that atheism is so attractive, but rather that religion is unattractive. Many would say that religion is actually the problem in the world today.

After 9/11 a number of books were written denouncing religion as the problem in the world. At the same time, in this country, a movement was underway, and a significant amount of people began to disconnect from church, religion, faith, and even God. So great was this movement away from God and religion that these people were given a name, they were called the "None's." These "None's" were unaffiliated with religion of any kind, and today make up about 23% of the population in this country. About 35% of millennials would say we're just not affiliated with anything religious. [2]

CHAPTER 2

A Creator

God's Paradigm

Skeptic and atheist publisher of *Skeptic Magazine*, Michael Shermer wrote that mankind is but a passing moment on the proscenium of the cosmos. The *Miriam-Webster Dictionary* Tells us that the proscenium is none other than the part of the stage in front of the curtain, between the curtain and the audience. We live our lives on the proscenium, the visible part of the stage. But as every devotee of the theater knows, the show is directed from behind the curtain. Out front on the stage of our lives, everything seems so simple, so easy to understand, like our salvation: trust in Jesus and receive the free gift of salvation. Yet when we go backstage, behind the curtain, the complexity is so amazing that it completely confounds the mind. That is the way God works: slowly, relentlessly, in the universe and in our lives. What I've written in this book is a tiny grain of sand on an immense beach compared to the total complexity of God's creation, and even this tiny grain of knowledge is nearly beyond our understanding. God has opened my eyes to this knowledge to share with you so that as you also step backstage, you get a small taste of His infinite creative abilities and what it required to bring you and I into existence as His beloved children. I never cease to marvel at His great love.

One might question why God neglected to include more information about the how of the Genesis creation, in particular how first life was brought about, something that might satisfy our curious, scientific minds. On the surface all we read is that "the Earth brought forth life." Not a very satisfactory description. But then who was He writing to? Well, 3,500 years ago, to Moses for one, and then of course to the Israelites. While Moses was most likely schooled in Pharaoh's court, he didn't have access to all of the scientific knowledge available today. So, it seems likely that God didn't include the fine details of how He created the universe and life on earth for obvious reasons: Can you imagine God trying to explain the big bang, DNA, gravity, time, and space to Moses, who in turn would have to explain the whole matter to the Israelites? It would most likely have led to complete chaos and the most important thing God was trying to communicate to them—that God is God and created the world—would have been hopelessly lost.

If the Bible was never intended to be *Science for Dummies*, what purpose does Genesis serve? I believe the Bible presents the story of God's interaction with the physical world He created from the very beginning through to the early development of the Christian church as brought about by His Son, Jesus the Christ. This narrative shows, through the lives of its characters, how God pursued a personal relationship with the humans He created. We see God repeatedly guide His people and show them His great love even to the death of His Son for the redemption of humankind. I believe this wonderful book is relevant from the very beginning in Genesis 1:1—"In the beginning God created the heavens and the earth"—to the very end in Revelations 22:18-19—"For I testify to everyone who hears the words of the prophecy of this book: If anyone adds to these things, God will add to him the plagues that are written in this book; and if anyone takes away from the words of the book of this prophecy, God shall take away his part from the Book of Life, from the holy city, and from the things which are written in this book."

I believe that God has always worked within a framework that He designed. According to the Bible, it all started when He acquired wisdom as the beginning of His way, the first of His works of old. Wisdom was established from everlasting, from the beginning, from before there ever was an earth. Wisdom, the totally metaphysical emanation from the Creator, yielded the big-bang creation of the physical universe in which we dwell. That tiny bit of energy created by God included all the intelligence required to bring and sustain life on this planet. It included all the RNA and DNA that would begin and control the various species and types of life on Earth, and all the physical and metaphysical laws that would govern the universe.

The Bible teaches us in Genesis 1:12, "And the earth brought forth grass, the herb that yields seed according to its kind, and the tree that yields fruit, whose seed is in itself according to its kind. And God saw that it was good." On the third day, when the environment on earth was suitable, it brought forth grass, herbs, and trees. I don't believe in the magical appearances of life on earth but rather that God is the author of order and that everything He did was planned and carried out in that order over billions of years, what Genesis talks about (according to Gerald Schroeder in the original Hebrew language) as six twenty-four-hour days. This is my understanding of what I find in His word and the discoveries of modern science, which are in complete agreement. Order is the fundamental process that God set up from the beginning and operates within. He can interject His own will through this same process and has throughout the history of the universe. It is still unfolding minute by minute, day by day, and year by year. He has a master overall plan that will be carried out as He chose from the very beginning of our world, yet He steps in as needed to make corrections when things get off track. He could have created this whole world in the blink of an eye but that isn't the way He chose to do it. God is in this for eternity, not just the present moment.

How Big Is God's Great Love?

In this century as well as those past, humans have used God's great gift: the ability to make great discoveries and begin the history making reconciliation between the science of creation and the word of God in Genesis. This has been accomplished through monumental strides in philosophy, mathematics, paleontology, cosmology, physics, biology, genetics, and astronomy. In fact, all the sciences participated in solving, both individually and together, many of the great mysteries that began at the creation of our universe. To name just a few, Einstein provided his understanding of the relativity of time, Planck had his discoveries of quantum mechanics, Penzias and Wilson defined cosmic background radiation, and genetics and the study of DNA showed us that the beginning of life on this planet was orchestrated by something far greater than Darwin's theory of evolution by random choice. Life would not exist without a guiding hand.

The Bible clearly states that God is sovereign, and that humankind has free will, the ability to make choices. Since God created everything from the same primordial dust of the universe, if humans have a free will, then so, in a sense, must nature, at least at the subatomic or quantum level. God built the universe with intelligence in every area, and He is a God of variety. Come, let us seek the thumbprint of God in science

CHAPTER 3

A Priori

Before our world came into existence there was **nothing**. No moon, no earth, no sun, no stars, no galaxies, nothing material existed, everything was void; not one thing existed, not even light or time, there wasn't even any space for there to be something in. But in all that nothingness there was God, and God had always, always, always been. There was never a time when God hasn't been. There were no clocks to record the eons of millennia that God has existed. God had no beginning; He simply always was. But you and I live in a material world where time does exist. We measure time with our clocks and we live our lives by those clocks. We operate in this world with our senses, and so it is beyond our comprehension to conceive there not being anything to see, touch, smell, hear, or taste. Our brain has no frame of reference, no way to grasp nonexistence, nothingness. How can someone, even God, exist where there is nothing, none of those sensory inputs we're surrounded with? But God is a spirit and has no need of light, air, space, or time. Those only exist in the material world we live in, the world He created for us.

William Lane Craig, world-renowned Christian philosopher and apologist describes God as He was before creation so aptly: "God is a perfect being, complete in Himself with no need of anything, with Him. There exists a perfect, changeless state of mutual knowledge, will and love among the persons of the Trinity without the creation. Creation, then, must be an act of grace, something done not for God's sake but for the sake of those created; namely, they are given the unspeakable opportunity to be personally related to the locus and source of infinite goodness and love. We were made to know God, and this is, in view of its object, an incommensurable good, incomparable to anything else, to any finite goods."[3]

Later in the same book Craig states that "the wonder of creation is that God would bother to create a world of creatures and invite them to freely enter the joy of that fellowship as adopted children!" That is the wonder, the mystery of God's grace, God's love, "and possibly why He created the universe!"[4]

God Had a Plan

In this chapter I have included scriptures as well as my thoughts and understanding of God's great love for humankind, humanity's predestination before creation, as well as God's existence outside of time. Some of what I have recorded here are random thoughts, whispers from God, and may not seem to flow from beginning to end but they are ideas and thoughts that I felt should somehow be brought together in this chapter and recorded.

Plans to populate His kingdom

Our hearts and minds are unable to understand, to fathom the depth, the width, the height, or the intensity of God's love for us, His creatures. We are incapable of grasping the lengths to which He will go to gain for us an entrance into His kingdom. One of the reasons I was compelled to write this book is to share with you my understanding of how great God's love for us is. My hope is that you will come away with a sense of what God did through the creation to secure your affection, how strongly He desires your love and presence in His life. God is a romantic, terribly in love with you. How can it be that He would give up His son to redeem us from destruction, from eternal death, and how can it be that His son, King of the universe, would leave His throne to take on the sins of the people He created, and die for us so that we might live with Him for eternity? As Phillip, Craig, and Dean sing, "Your grace still amazes me, your love still a mystery."[5]

The following scripture gives us an idea of how great God's love was before he even created His universe. We read in 2 Tim. 1:9-10: "God, who has saved us and called us with a holy calling, not according to our works, but according to His own purpose and grace which was given to us in Christ Jesus before time began, but has now been revealed by the appearing of our Savior Jesus Christ, who has abolished death and brought life and immortality to light through the gospel."

Before the creation there was only God and within Him was the mystery of His love for us and His desire that we have eternal life, which would be brought about through His Son, our savior. According to the Bible we were in God's plan before time existed, but with the creation God brought time into existence and revealed his plan through Jesus Christ. Hopefully this book will give you a glimpse inside that grace, that mystery.

God and Time

Long before the creation became a reality, I believe the triune God determined to populate a heavenly realm with a kingdom ruled by His Son. But who were to be His loyal subjects? God doesn't have to gain knowledge; He already has all knowledge. He has always been able to know or foreknow the future. But God knowing the future does not mean He determines the future; just that He knows what will happen. Therefore, God has no impact on our free will; we are free to choose as we will. How was He able to do this before the creation? Louis Jacobs explains it thusly: "God doesn't exist in our time continuum; He exists outside of time. He does not know the future because He foresees its occurrence, but because it is no more removed from Him than the past or present" ... One of the names the Torah employs to refer to God consists of the Hebrew letters yud-hey-yuv-hey... These letters constitute a contracted form of the Hebrew words *was-is-will be.* and conveys the sense of God's eternality, not in the sense that He exists forever but in that He is above time altogether.

God has perfect knowledge; He has no need to gain knowledge. He knows the totality of everything that has ever occurred in the lives of every person ever conceived in this world. He has the complete knowledge of everything that has ever happened or will happen in our lives, past, present, and future, every decision we will make, and because He exists outside of time, He is able to see the complete panorama of each one of our lives as one scene, from conception to death.

However, knowing something will happen is not the same as making it happen. While God knows fully what will happen in each of our lives, and even though He may affect some of those events, His knowledge does not determine those events or what decisions we will make. We cannot confuse His foreknowledge with a timeless determination of those events. God's timeless knowledge of what will occur in the created realm must be worked out in time for it to become a reality. We do not do what God foreknows. God's foreknowledge is not the cause of our actions; our actions are the cause of His foreknowledge.

The reason I have been going through this exercise in foreknowledge is that, to me, it plays an important part in God's precreation plans as we look at predestination. Reading in Romans

8:28 "And we know that all things work together for good to those who love God, to those who are the called according to His purpose, for whom He foreknew, He also predestined to be conformed to the image of His Son that He might be the firstborn among many brethren. Moreover, whom He predestined, these He also called, whom He called, these He also justified; and whom He justified these He also glorified." And as well in Eph. 1:4-5: "just as He chose us in Him before the foundation of the world, that we should be holy and without blame before Him in love, having predestined us to adoption as sons by Jesus Christ to himself according to the good pleasure of His will." And finally, in I Tim. 2:19: "Nevertheless the solid foundation of God stands, having this seal. The Lord knows those who are His."

God and the Universe: An Interesting Perspective

Before the creation of the world (i.e., the cosmos or universe), God knew who His people would be by looking at their whole life. There is no future in God's world because there is no time. So, anything He does is only in His world not ours until it happens, something He was able to do without changing anything they would do He foreknew who would trust Him as well as who wouldn't. That is, those who would accept Christ as Lord and savior somewhere during their lives. And those who He saw as receiving Christ during their lives he chose and predestined to be conformed to the Son. Those are the people He chose to populate His future kingdom of which His son the Christ is King.

Before the big bang, before the universe was created, God had already selected those who would be joining him for eternity in the celestial city. "I think it possible that God designed the new Earth mentioned in the book of Revelation with those people in mind, those who would join him in eternity. The Bible does not necessarily support this idea directly, but I can see it as an expression of

God's intense love for us. Of course, we must still live our lives out, but God already has the knowledge of how our life began, what it was about, and how it ended. He knows our lives from one end to the other. This chapter represents something I have thought about for some time."[6]

The New Testament tells us that the universe was created by and for the Son of God. He left His throne, His kingdom, to become a small Jewish baby, grow up, and be put to death on a cross by those same people He came to save, to die for the sins of those He created, so they would be acceptable to His Father, and become part of His kingdom, living with Him for eternity. We are so deeply indebted to our God; Father, Son, and Holy Spirit. That in itself is hard to grapple with, hard to get our minds around, and yet His Love and Grace continue to cover us every moment of our lives. God just keeps on giving and giving and giving. The only way we can even begin to repay Him is to love Him and serve Him for eternity. "You shall Love the Lord your God with all your heart, with all your soul and with all your mind. This is the first and great commandment. And the second is like it: You shall love your neighbor as yourself." (Matt. 22:37-39)

According to science we are made from the very stardust of the universe that was created from the big bang. All those elemental particles that began in the early expansion of the universe and are still in existence, stuff that scientists are still scratching their heads over. Is it possible these tiny subatomic particles are what keep the universe balanced and operating? Will they be used to create the bodies belonging to the children of the kingdom of God? Some of these particles can travel at speeds close to the velocity of light. Many can pass through structures, the sun, and stars without bumping into anything. Because of time dilation it would take hardly any time to reach the closest stars. These thoughts open interesting possibilities.

CHAPTER 4

A Beginning

According to the Old Testament scriptures, God created the universe with His wisdom, knowledge and understanding. I take this literally, that wisdom played a major role in the creation, and particularly in programming the big bang that science says began the universe. I have come to this conclusion from examining scripture and both the early Jewish commentaries and the writings of Gerald L. Schroeder, an Orthodox Jewish scholar and MIT professor of physics. To me this process not only fits with scripture but makes complete sense with my understanding of how God works. Again, this may conflict with your understanding of how God created the universe but hopefully it gives you something to ponder.

God's wisdom is a far-reaching, multidimensional subject. What humankind knows about God's wisdom can fill many libraries, yet if the whole of God's wisdom could be written, there probably isn't enough space in this universe to hold all the volumes. We live our lives by the wisdom God shared through Solomon and Paul, who wrote so much about the wisdom of Christ, yet we still know so little about it. But the wisdom I am going to share with you in this chapter focuses on what was used in the building of God's universe, our Earth, and all that lives and exists on this planet.

God's wisdom is at the core of how He put it all together, from the first tiny drop of intense energy in the Big Bang to the complexity of a human mind in the body of Adam. That's a lot of information, much more than our finite minds can process. So, I will limit what I share in this chapter and yet include enough to give you a picture of how great our God is, plus an idea how He might have worked through the creation to generate life, and how wisdom in the creation enabled free will for both humans and nature.

As I was working my way through each of the many books I read prior to beginning this writing, each day I was so amazed by the extent God went to in order to bring about life on this planet. It really is almost unbelievable, the detail required just to balance our solar system within the Milky Way galaxy and perfectly position all the planets, our sun, and moon so that life could exist and flourish on Earth. The required accuracy is so critical that there was no room for error. It couldn't have been by accident that it all came out this way.[7]

We know, from reading the New Testament, that God planned all along that His Son, our King, would be the creating agent to bring all of this about. According to Paul in Col. 1:16, "For by Him all things were created that are in heaven and that are on earth, visible and invisible, whether thrones or dominions or principalities or powers. All things were created through Him and for Him." Then in Hebrews 1:1-2, Paul writes again that "God…has in these last days spoken to us by His son, whom He has appointed heir of all things, through whom also He made the worlds." And in the gospel of John 1:3-4, we read that "All things were made through Him, and without Him nothing was made that was made. In Him was life, and the life was the light of men." Obviously, these passages are talking about the son of God being the creative agent of God.

The first thing that God created was the wisdom that would bring the new universe into being, and must have been required in order to program the tiny spot of energy that would become all that is now in the universe. Speaking about the wisdom used in the creation, Solomon says, "The Lord by wisdom founded the earth; by understanding He established the heavens; by His knowledge the depths were broken up, and clouds drop down the dew" in Proverbs 3:19. And in Proverbs 8:22-31, he continues

"The Lord possessed me at the beginning of His way, Before His works of old. I have been established from everlasting. From the beginning, before there was ever an earth. When there were no depths, I was brought forth, when there were no fountains abounding with water. Before the mountains were settled. Before the hills, I was brought forth; while as yet He had not made the earth or the outer places or the primal dust of the world. When He prepared the heavens, I was there. When He drew a circle on the face of the deep, when He established the clouds above, when He strengthened the fountains of the deep, when He assigned to the sea its limit, so that the waters would not transgress His command, when He marked out the foundations of the earth, then I was beside Him as a master craftsman; and I was daily His delight, rejoicing always before Him, rejoicing in His inhabited world, and my delight was with the sons of men."

Wisdom is ubiquitous, the substrate of every particle of the world and most evident in the brains and minds of humans as we discover our cosmic origins. The success of life is indeed, written into the fabric of the universe.

The King James Bible, first published in 1611, translated from the Latin Vulgate and the Greek Septuagint translates Genesis 1:1 as "In the beginning God created the heaven and the earth." According to OT scholar Gerald Schroeder this translation loses some of the meaning captured in the original Hebrew. The first word in Hebrew, *B'reasheat*, can be translated as "In the beginning of." The problem is that the preposition "of" there has no subject, so the translators just dropped it in the KJV. But the 2,100-year-old Jerusalem translation into Aramaic interprets this somewhat different. Realizing that B'reasheet is a compound word—the prefix *B'* (with) and *reasheet* (first wisdom)—the Aramaic translation is thus "With wisdom God created the heavens and the earth." Reading through Proverbs 8, and in particular 8:22-23, which speaking about wisdom "The Lord possessed me at the beginning of His way, Before His works of old. I have been established from everlasting," The Jerusalem translation makes sense, and opens a window to reveal how wisdom played a role in the early creation, and matches up with scripture.[8]

Reading each of these quotes, including the scriptures, I must conclude that from the very beginning, the Son imparted the wisdom of God into the tiny spot of energy that produced the universe. God's wisdom permeated every part of the universe through the quantum subatomic particles, photons, protons, neutrons, electrons, and quarks that came as a result of the energy from the big bang to create all the laws of nature, all the stars, galaxies, planets suns, moons asteroids, everything that consists of matter today. When Earth came into being, it consisted of the material generated from billions of years of stars bursting and generating stardust that flew throughout the universe and began to form more planets, stars, and galaxies as gravity began to pull the particles together. Everything in the universe was made from that stardust, including you and me, and in that stardust was the wisdom of God. We are the result of God's wisdom and stardust. From the dust Adam was formed, as was all life—the stardust of the universe that came from the wisdom of God. And within that wisdom that created the universe, according to Dr. Schroeder, was the *tzim tzum*, or freedom to make choices.[9]

In every piece and aspect of the world we find wisdom. As bizarre as it may seem, the world, in a very real sense, has a mind of its own. To understand how that dynamic force manifests itself in the ever-changing created world, we turn to the only two relevant sources of information: nature—that is, the world around us—and the Bible. Both provide confirmation that God's essence is as vibrant as the world itself. In this sense, the study of nature is as much a study of God as the study of the Bible is. As Ps. 19:1 says, "The heavens declare the glory of God; And the firmament shows His handiwork." God reveals His creativity in the grandeur of galactic space as well as in the details of an atom. From both realms, though they differ vastly in dimension, we can learn how God acts in this world He created. In Romans 1:20, Paul states that "For since the creation of the world His invisible attributes are clearly seen, being understood by the things that are made, even His eternal power and Godhead, so that they are without excuse." Paul seemed to be saying that it should be obvious from looking about us that neither chance nor a mere human could have made something like this universe. And that if we look closely enough, we should be able to visualize the attributes of God; His power, love, and intelligence from nature,

As an example, so precise was the intelligence of the creation, we ourselves are the most complex, advanced supercomputers in existence. As Schroeder states, "The human body acts as a finely tuned machine, a magnificent metropolis in which, as its inhabitants, each of the 75 trillion cells, composed of 10^{27} atoms, moves in symbiotic precision. Seldom are two cells simultaneously performing the same act, yet their individual contributions combine smoothly to form life."[10]

In chapter 5 we look at free will and provide answers as to why God built choice into the universe.

CHAPTER 5

A Choice

Free Will – Choosing Pleasure and the Disruption It Has Caused

"The only unalterable destiny in life is that life itself is a continual crossroads of choice, and the driving force behind that choice is the search for what we perceive as pleasure. Mistaking short-term gratification for transcendental pleasure is something like confusing infatuation with love. How much misery has been founded on that error? But then, immediate pleasure is so tempting." That mankind would desire immediate pleasure was programmed into the DNA along with survival, from the beginning, and of course other basic urges like sex, anger, hunger, success etc. etc. Some of these things are what make us different from other animals. Without these urges to motivate us we probably wouldn't have lasted as long as we have nor advanced as far. But along with the good they have brought about there is also a negative side to each of these urges. There is the possibility of abuse which has most likely been active since the Big Bang in the whole universe, but particularly in mankind.[11]

Right from the beginning, in Genesis, we see how God gave (and humankind abused) free will: And along with free will came the choice of disobeying God for Adam and Eve, and with that disobedience sin, or *missing the mark* in the Hebrew.

> "And the Lord God planted a garden eastward in Eden, and there he put Adam.... And the Lord God made grow every tree that is pleasant to the sight and good for food; the tree of life within the garden and also the tree of the knowledge of good and evil.... And the Lord God commanded Adam saying of every tree of the garden you may certainly eat but of the tree of the knowledge of good and evil you may not eat, for in the day that you eat of it you shall surely die.... When the woman (Eve) saw that the tree was good for food and that it was tempting to the eyes and suited to make one wise, she took from its fruit and gave it to her man with her and he ate." Genesis 2:8,9,16-17, 3::1-24

> * The Bible: The Holy Scriptures. Jerusalem: Koren Publishers, 1969. (Hebrew and English) or The Babylonian Talmud. Transl. from the original Hebrew and Aramaic into English. London: Soncino Press, 1977.

"I, wisdom, was with the Lord when he began his work, long before he made anything else. I was created in the very beginning, even before the world began." Proverbs 8:22-23. * According to Kabala logic (the ancient study by Jewish believers of how God interacts with His creation), when God created wisdom, He withdrew enough to allow free will to be a part of that wisdom. This process was known as "*tzim tzum*, the Hebrew word for contraction."[12]

According to the Bible, Genesis 3 is the first example of mankind disobeying Gods command, although it is not the first example of Adam making choices of his own. Earlier in Genesis God brought various creatures to Adam and instructed him to give them names. That being said, I feel it is part of the story to look at the first example of disobedience in the Bible and the trouble it has caused mankind and the world as it appears in Genesis chapter 3.

> "Now the serpent was more cunning than any beast of the field which the Lord God had made. And he said to the woman, 'Has God indeed said, you shall not eat of every tree of the garden'? And the woman said to the serpent, 'We may eat the fruit of the trees of the garden; but of the fruit of the tree which *is* in the midst of the garden, God has said,' 'You shall not eat it, nor shall you touch it, lest you die.' Then the serpent said to the woman, 'You will not surely die. For God knows that in the day you eat of it your eyes will be opened, and you will be like God, knowing good and evil.' So, when the woman saw that the tree *was* good for food, that it *was* pleasant to the eyes, and a tree desirable to make *one* wise, she took of its fruit and ate. She also gave to her husband with her, and he ate. Then the eyes of both of them were opened, and they knew that they *were* naked; and they sewed fig leaves together and made themselves coverings."

In this scripture I found it Interesting to note that though Adam and Eve actually had a free will to obey or disobey God before eating the fruit, the serpent said "you shall be like God knowing good and evil." They had a free will to make decisions, but they didn't know the difference between good and evil in their hearts until they disobeyed God. This leads me to propose the question, is it possible to have a free will yet not know evil, which was first manifest in the person of the serpent. An interesting thought to consider for our future life on the other side.

Gen. 4:1–5, 8

And Adam knew his wife, and she became pregnant and gave birth to Cain saying, I have acquired a man from the Eternal. And again, she gave birth, to his brother, Abel. And Abel was a shepherd and Cain was a worker of the soil. And in time it came to pass that Cain brought from the fruit of the soil an offering to the Eternal. And Abel, he also brought from the first born of the flock and the fat parts thereof and the Eternal accepted Abel and his offering; but to Cain and his offering the Eternal did not accept, and Cain was very angry . . . .. And it came to pass when they (Cain and Abel) were in the field that Cain rose up against Abel

According to the Bible, by the third chapter in Genesis Adam and Eve had already disobeyed God and brought sorrow and pain into their lives, and by the fourth chapter their son Cain had murdered his brother and been marked for life. In a world where humankind was given free will, bad things were going to happen, even to people who were good. God could have stopped Cain from killing his brother, but He didn't because that would have been inconsistent with the free will He gave to humankind.

So, what is the answer to the disruption caused by free will? God could have constructed humans with their brains less oriented toward misuse of those attributes, but according to genetic science if He had, a vital part of the human brain God created, that brain that seeks to accomplish and dominate his world, would have been missing, and humans would not have had "dominion over the fish of the sea, over the birds of the air, and over the cattle, over all the earth and over every creeping thing that creeps on the earth" (Gen. 1:26b). Our free will—the same feature that enables us to create and perform atrocities and destroy the world—also allows us to take dominion over it, as God commanded. And while it was not God's plan that humans commit evil, it was not something that could be avoided if we were to have a free will, even though it would reign catastrophe on the world. Free will was obviously in God's plan from the beginning in spite of the problems it would cause.

Nature's Role in Tragedy

If all suffering were attributable to human agency, then free will and our inherent ability to err might seem more logical. Unfortunately, the blind forces of nature lie behind nearly as much human grief as humans themselves. An earthquake, a tsunami, a landslide, tornado, or hurricane can instantly take thousands of lives; children are born with defective hearts; both drought and monsoon cause famine. What we must realize is that this is also part of God's wise design: "Consider the work of God; For who can make straight what He has made crooked? In the day of prosperity be joyful, but in the day of adversity consider: Surely God has appointed the one as well as the other, so that man can find out nothing that will come after him" (Ecclesiastes 7:13-14). As we can see from this verse (and know from observing the world around us), The same Creator that produces the beauty of a sunrise and the colors of a flower must be credited with these horrors as well.[13]

Free Will and Quantum Physics

According to Orthodox Jewish physicist Gerald Schroeder, Scientists have been studying about free will under the guise of quantum physics during the past 100 years or so., but only recently has the study of quantum physics captured the attention of the world. As humans we experience our three-dimensional physical world of length, width, and depth as well as the dimensions of time and space, yet physicists now tell us that there could be as many as twenty-six dimensions to our universe; that our "solid" world is actually 99.9999999999999 percent empty space made solid by hypothetical, force-carrying, massless particles; and that those tiny insignificant amounts of matter may not actually be matter, but wavelets of energy that we material beings sense as matter. This is the world of quantum physics."[14]

The physics for free will in nature may be at the quantum level. Quantum mechanics teaches that while the general path of a reaction may be predictable, the exact path is not. There is a probabilistic spread in the path that connects cause to effect. That divergence opens a window of opportunity for what might be choice." Scientists have tried coming up with a natural set of laws that can explain the action, origin, reason, and result of sub atomic particles such as quarks, and neutrino's as well as other particles but have found that they don't always follow consistent behavioral patterns. And while we know that nature is relatively predictable, quantum particles are not. [15]

Here is one description of quantum mechanics (another term for quantum physics or quantum theory): Quantum mechanics provides a mathematical description of much of the dual particle-like and wave-like behavior and interactions of energy and matter. Much more simply stated, things that can't be explained by the known laws of nature happen in nature at a subatomic level between energy and matter. Yes, nature often operates outside its own laws in the subatomic world of atoms and quarks, which leaves scientists scratching their heads. So, they call these unexplained phenomena quantum physics. Obviously, this is an oversimplification of a relatively new, very complex metaphysical branch of science, but the bottom line is that known science cannot explain everything that happens in our universe. This should come as no surprise to believers though, as God already tells us in Isaiah 55:9

that "as the heavens are higher than the earth, so are my ways higher than your ways, and my thoughts than your thoughts."

Free Choice – The Reflection of God

Interestingly, we know from Exodus that when Moses was confronted by God, he questioned Him, asking God who he should say gave him the message he was to take back to the Israelites. Moses wanted to know what name he should call God by. According to the English translations of Exodus 3:14, "God said to Moses, 'I AM WHO I AM.' And He said, 'Thus you shall say to the children of Israel, 'I AM' has sent you." However, the Hebrew actually has God saying to Moses, "ehe'ye ehe'ye,"* which more accurately translates to "I will be that which I will be."[16]

Just as God is not predictable or static, neither is His creation, for we are His reflection. This morning a thought occurred to me that while we may learn new things about God from science as well as the Bible and this knowledge may change how we think about or perceive God, God Himself hasn't changed. Whether the information we learn is right or wrong, it may change us, but God remains the same as He has ever been, regardless of what we learn or believe, and that was a comfort to me. God is allowed to change His mind or course of action but He always operates on the basis of His attributes, and His love for us.

The Bible defines the result of free choice in the first five books only once, in Deuteronomy 30:19, and the choice is between life and death: "I call heaven and earth as witnesses today against you, that I have set before you life and death, blessing and cursing; therefore, choose life that both you and your descendants may live." With each act of tzim tzum, the Bible tells us, the channel through which all of nature flows broadened. Its license to meander increased. As mentioned earlier in this chapter the tzimtzum was God's way of stepping back during the creation to allow flexibility for all of nature, including mankind, for free choice.

These Bible translations are taken from one of the following sources: The Bible: The Holy Scriptures. Jerusalem: Koren Publishers, 1969. (Hebrew and English) or The Babylonian Talmud. Transl. from the original Hebrew and Aramaic into English. London: Soncino Press, 1977.

CHAPTER 6

A Matter of Matter

What Was the Universe Created From?

According to Christian apologist and theologian William Lane Craig: Christian theology is committed to the doctrine that God created the universe, and that it was created when nothing material existed. The Latin term *ex nihilo*, which means out of nothing. No previous energy or material substance was used. The Bible confirms this in Genesis 1:1 which says that "In the beginning God *created* the heavens and the earth." According to Old Testament theologian and former MIT professor, Gerald Schroeder, "the word "created" is the Hebrew word *Barah*. It is the only word in the Hebrew language that means the creation of something from nothing, and it is used only to describe the actions of God in creation."[17]

God used only His wisdom to create the energy required by the big bang, yet this tiny spot of intensely hot and dense energy became the entire universe. There was no material used, as there could have been no material in a timeless existence. The only thing required was the agent, the Son of God.

Roger Penrose, professor of mathematics at Oxford University, with expertise in the study of the early universe was awarded the Wolf Prize for his description of the Big Bang which has become the bases of early cosmology. According to Penrose the Big Bang was the beginning of the universe described as a very tiny spot of intense energy heated to an incredibly high temperature. According to the Bible that tiny spot of intense energy was created by God from nothing. [18]

Scientists say that anything before the Big Bang is beyond the realm of science since there was nothing scientific to analyze or study. Those that subscribe to the Big Bang agree that almost immediately after the initial explosion of the big bang, the universe was a black hole held together by intense gravity but in the next instant began to expand at a very high speed, reaching the speed of light in seconds, (see The First 3 Minutes).

It all began with only super-heated gasses until the temperature dropped enough for matter to form. As soon as that happened, time and light were created, and space began stretching until a massive nebula formed. Even today, space is still stretching, and the universe is still expanding. According to scientists of astronomy, the formation of stars and galaxies took more time, perhaps billions of years. Over many eons these stars formed, imploded, then exploded, sending stardust throughout the universe to again form new stars, galaxies, and solar systems. This is how Earth eventually was formed, from stardust.

From this auspicious beginning matter throughout the universe was created and became what we see in the stars in the sky and the earth we live upon. A number of the following chapters further explain the creation of matter from different aspects.

A New Science

On the surface, traditional physics was always able to logically predict cause and effect. The laws and principals of physics always produced the same results. These are basic laws and principles that have been in effect forever, studied and demonstrated by early physicists, and for the most part they deal with nature that is easily seen and studied.

All that began to change early in the twentieth century when a new breed of scientists came along: Einstein and his theory that time was relative to speed and gravity; Max Planck and his quantum theory on atomic and subatomic processes; Louis de Broglie, who suggested that matter actually had wave properties as well as physical properties; and Werner Karl Heisenberg's uncertainty principle and theory of quantum mechanics. And then theoretical physics jumped ahead and started declaring that the subatomic particles we thought we were familiar with weren't round ping-pong balls like we previously thought, but rather more like waves of information than anything else. These statements may leave you wondering if anything is what it seems, and a possible answer to that question according to scientists is probably not, at least when you get to the subatomic quantum world.

Our sensory world

We live in a sensory world and our sensors pick up on "material" objects no matter what they are made of, but God could have made us differently so that we sensed waves and frequencies, and that would have been a whole different world. The reason I say this is that the duality of matter can be sensed as material as well as waves or frequencies. And if we think about it, while we respond and understand waves and frequencies such as light and sound, our whole outlook on life is oriented towards material substances. We live in houses, drive cars, grow food, most everything we experience daily involves matter. I know there must be reason He created our world with that duality but understanding why is far beyond my ability. While quantum physics tells us that everything is made of both subatomic particles from matter and waves, we live in a material world where we see and touch material things even though they also exist as waves and frequencies.

We can thank Albert Einstein for much of this advancement with his theory of relativity, a theory which has since been proven scientifically correct. In his formula Einstein states that m (for matter) intrinsically represented a specific amount of energy (E), and the type of energy is immaterial. As bizarre as it seems, a gram of rose petals and gram of uranium contain identical amounts of energy. The constant (C^2) in the formula represents the speed of light squared or multiplied by itself. That C^2 is a massive value tells us that even a tiny amount of matter contains a huge quantity of latent energy, and this leads us to the Big Bang theory where physicists claim it all started. There are of course other theories, but the big bang theory seems to be the most widely accepted model today.

God is so amazing to have thought up all of this wonder in order to create a universe, a home, just for us. Could there ever be a greater love expressed to finite beings like us? Sometimes I get so caught up in all of this scientific wonder that I have to step back and get a bigger perspective. That is where I am right now. In my soul I know that there is a purpose for all of this, and that there is a God so filled with love that He spared no expense in creating a home for His creatures. The wonder of it all is that He could have just as easily created a complete, packaged, perfect universe and placed us in it, but He did not. Our God does not work that way. He could but He does not. The world is incredibly complex just as we are complex beings, and that complexity took a long time to form. We cover that in more depth in the following chapters.

CHAPTER 7

An Explanation Time, Light, Matter, Space Gravity

Before God began His process of creating the universe there was absolutely nothing except God; no time, light, matter, space, and no gravity. All these things we take completely for granted because they are what we live in, but they weren't in existence then. When God began creating the universe, He required light, time, gravity, and space in order to create matter, galaxies, our solar system, Earth, and life. None of the creation could exist without them, which was how He had planned it. God was the master planner and creator; He knew exactly what was needed to bring life and humankind into existence. In this chapter we discuss the first light, time, gravity, and space as created by God at the very beginning of the universe.

Before Time Began

In this section William Lane Craig, American Christian apologist and teacher proposes an explanation from his own thinking that relates God to the time before and after He began the creation of the universe.

91 Allow me to state succinctly my understanding of God's relationship to time. I argue that God, existing changelessly alone without the universe, is timeless (there was no such thing as time before the creation). Time comes into existence at creation and so has a beginning and is finite (nonexistent) in the past. God, in virtue of His real relationship to the temporal world, becomes temporal at the moment of creation. So, God exists timelessly without creation and temporally since the moment of creation. (This sounds complicated but really isn't. God existed without time before the creation but because the universe He created has matter time must exist and therefore in order for God to relate to us in this physical universe He must also take on a temporal or worldly aspect. For example, He became the burning bush when Moses sought him in Egypt.) If I am right, then there is no moment prior to creation. Rather, time begins at creation. This is the classical Christian view, as defended, for example, by Augustine. On this view, it is logically incoherent to ask, 'What was God doing prior to creation?' because 'prior to creation' implies a moment before creation, which the view denies," and prior to the creation there was no time.[19]

Obviously, this presents a real conundrum because there is really no way to discuss what God was doing prior to the creation. However, for the purpose of this book I will refer to things that occurred before time existed just as the bible does. For example, many scriptures refer to God existing before He began the creation and, in some cases, even what He was doing before the creation.

Light as the cosmic clock for measuring time

Everyday clocks rely on spring mechanisms or household electricity, which in this country is generated at approximately 60 cycles per second (or hertz) per second. The sundial for many centuries has been a method used to tell the time of day, however it does not measure amounts of time accurately. While these methods for keeping track of time are satisfactory for most use, scientists require both the keeping track of and measuring of time to be far more accurate. A more stable and accurate way to keep track of and measure time was found by utilizing the frequency of light. This is possible because the speed of light is stable and consistent throughout the universe at 300 million meters per second in a vacuum. In this manner time and light are related to each other, although not directly. There are other factors that also play a part in determining time throughout the universe as are discussed in the next section.

Because "Light has the mysterious property of being both a particle and a wave. (As in frequency sine wave) It is the wave aspect that allows us to measure time over cosmic distances. What we refer to as visible light is only one particular band of wavelengths (or frequency) in a nearly infinite range of electromagnetic radiations (or frequencies) all of which travel at the same speed,"[25] which is 300 million meters per second in a vacuum. Although the frequency of light is variable, depending upon what wavelength, the speed of that light is consistent, and completely reliable "Our application of light in calculating the passage of time on the Sun relative to the Earth demonstrated the usefulness of light frequency as a cosmic clock."[20]

The Early Clock of the Universe based on CBR

Cosmic rays are a form of high-energy radiation found throughout the universe that produces measurable frequencies. One of these frequencies in particular was discovered in 1965 by two scientists, Arno Penzias and Robert Wilson. They proposed that this cosmic background radiation (CBR) has been present and ubiquitous throughout the universe since the creation. Scientists now call this particular frequency the remnant or echo of the big bang. This CBR frequency has been determined to be the basis of cosmic time and is now called the clock of Genesis: We will discuss this Universal Time further in later chapters.

Light

Genesis 1:2–4 says, "The earth was without form, and void; and darkness was on the face of the deep. And the Spirit of God was hovering over the face of the waters. Then God said, 'Let there be light'; and there was light. And God saw the light, that it was good; and God divided the light from the darkness." Science tells us that the first moment of light occurred between 240,000 and 300,000 years after the big bang: and this is the scientific explanation of how that happened.

When the temperature fell below 3000°K, a critical event occurred: Light separated from matter and emerged from the darkness of the universe. However, the 'light' of Genesis 1:3 existed prior to the Divine separation of light from darkness, which is described in Genesis 1:4. Both the Talmud and cosmology acknowledge that this first 'light' was of a nature so powerful that it would not have been visible by humans. Science tells us that the 'light' of that early period was in the energy range of gamma rays, an energy far in excess of that which is visible to the eye. This allowed electrons to bind in stable orbits around hydrogen and helium nuclei. Not only did the photons break free from the matter of the universe according to Genesis 1:4 the Torah notes that light was separated from darkness and became visible as well. Light (in the universe) was now light and darkness dark, theologically and scientifically. While this may, or may not make sense to you as a reader, it does provide further explanation of the Biblical claim that God separated the light from the darkness; the overall process that occurred from the beginning of earth's development with regard to light. The following explanation, according to astronomers and physicists, provides a more scientific explanation for this separation between light and darkness. With an understanding that light was actually held within the primeval mass until being freed by the binding of electrons into atomic orbits, the enigmatic division by God between light (which is totally composed of photons) and darkness takes on a significance consistent with its literal meaning. In other words, light was separated from darkness when all of the photon atoms were complete causing light to be visible.

Matter

A Retranslation of Genesis 1:2 "And the earth was Tohu and bohu… (Gen. 1:2). The usual translation of this verse from the book of Genesis is, And the earth was unformed (Tohu) and void (bohu). Unformed or chaotic is a fair translation of tohu. But bohu does not only mean void. Both the Talmud and Nialamides state that bohu means filled with the building blocks of matter."[21]

Additionally, less than 100 years ago nuclear physicists found that the real world was less solid than we thought. "Who would have dreamt that the solid world is really 99.9999999999999 percent empty space made solid by hypothetical, force-carrying, massless particles? And that even that minuscule fraction of matter that is matter may not actually be matter, but wavelets of energy that we material beings' sense as matter? Absurd as these principles seem to the human mind, the universe we have discovered behaves in a manner most illogical.

Since biblical time takes hold with the appearance of matter, the biblical clock starts at bohu, that instant just after the big bang when stable matter as we know it formed from energy. The age of all matter in the universe dates back to bohu, the moment of quark confinement (or singularity). We know the temperature and hence the frequency of radiation energy in the universe at quark confinement…. That radiant energy had a frequency a million million times greater than the radiation of today's (CBR) cosmic background radiation. The radiation from that moment of quark confinement has been stretched a million-millionfold…. That stretching of the light waves has slowed the frequency of the cosmic clock…expanded the perceived time between ticks of that clock, by a million. I use and further describe CBR in the chapter titled "A Different Perspective or Frame of Reference" because I use it to explain time dilation for calculating the difference in biological time (15 billion years) versus God's universe time (six 24-hour days), and will also be used in the chapter titled "Harmony between Modern Science and the Bible.

The Problem with Dinosaurs and the Bible

Stepping back in time to the 6th 24-hour day when God brought forth living creatures. According to science that day lasted approximately 250 million years and it was during that period dinosaurs came into being as part of the living creatures the earth brought forth. Those creatures during the Mesozoic Era, dinosaurs ruled Earth for 120 million years, as measured by our perception of time. Those clocks are set by the decay of radioactive nuclides here on Earth and they are correct for our earthly system. But to know the cosmic time (see the following paragraph for an explanation of why the earth clock was different than the cosmic time) we must divide earth time by a million million. At this million-million-to-one ratio those 120 million Earth years would have lasted a mere hour. For those who wonder why the Bible doesn't mention the period of the dinosaurs, it seems unimportant to record something that lasted one mere hour by the clock of the Universe, and even though dinosaurs make for interesting movies, their short one-hour lifetime by the clock of the universe (1 of 144 hours) relegates them to nonplayers in the overall scope of the creation. However, they are important in that they are a part of the 6th day when the Earth brought forth animal life, but not any more important than any of the other millions of living creatures save Adam.

Measuring the age of the universe using today's Earth-based clock indicates that the universe is billions of years old. But that isn't the clock of the universe, which was a composite of all locations in the early universe and measured time a million million times slower. The clock of the early universe was based on the CBR present at the of time the big bang and is the clock used to measure the six 24-hour days recorded in Genesis. While that cosmic time piece measures one minute, an equivalent earth-based clock measures a million million minutes. As the universe grew, radiation stretched, and gravity changed until the cosmic clock was ticking at the same rate as the earth clock.

Space

Space is the expanse that exists between celestial bodies. It is not empty or filled with air but consists of a hard vacuum containing a low density of particles, predominantly hydrogen and helium plasma and electromagnetic radiation, magnetic fields, elemental particles, neutrinos, dust, and cosmic rays. (With the creation of time and matter, space was created and continuous to expand even though there is nothing physical outside of space) because space as we know it ends at the edge of the universe. We may close the door to a room, but we are well aware that the space on the other side of the door continues to exist. We are familiar only with the sort of boundary that has something on the other side.

According to scientists of astronomy, the universe is expanding and has been since the Big Bang billions of years ago. Additionally, there is no known limit to how large the universe can be. It started out not existing and came into being at the big bang, therefore it is finite (i.e., with measurable limits) rather than being infinite (i.e., without limits or boundaries). There are those who suppose the universe, along with time and space, has always existed and that it is infinite, something way beyond our ability to comprehend. But that is not the theistic view, which asserts that the universe had a definite beginning and remains finite yet ever-expanding.

Gravity

Very little is known about gravity other than when it started and how it affects the universe. Books are filled with information about gravity, how it affects light, and matter, but not how it works which is still somewhat of a mystery. It was required from the beginning of the creation in order for masses to coalesce and form stars, galaxies, solar systems, and planets, and of course is still required on our planet. The closest anyone has come to understanding or describing gravity was Albert Einstein, who proposed in his general theory of relativity that gravity was a consequence of the curvature of spacetime caused by the uneven distribution of mass. This description is generally accepted by modern physics, although it is way beyond my own comprehension.

We take gravity for granted, because we know that if we drop a rock it falls toward the earth. But scientists have not been able to understand gravity. They know it exists but not how it exists? Without some amount of gravity across the whole universe, there would be no stars, no Milky Way, no Earth, and no humankind or life. Gravity was part of the wisdom of God, part of His plan. To believers, gravity doesn't need to be explained, just accepted as one of the amazing forces created by God to form the universe and keep us from flying off into space.

CHAPTER 8

A Moment or Two

The First Few Minutes of the Universe

I added this section to help us grasp the immensity of the creation, and in particular that first few moments of its existence; when from absolutely nothing, God created a cataclysmic explosion so immense, so spectacular, that it included all of the matter necessary to create the billions of heavenly bodies that exist today, and continues to expand, according to Hubble and NASA, at the incredible rate of over 150,000 miles per hour and is actually increasing in speed. Some of the numbers you will read in this chapter may be hard to get your head wrapped around. Enter the world God lives in.

The Bible neither explains the detailed process of how the universe exploded, from what elements it was made, or how fast it increased in size. It merely states that in the beginning God created the heavens and the earth. Evidently no further explanation was required to convince humankind at that time how God accomplished this feat. Science books are filled with various suppositions how it all unfolded. But these are all pretty much guesses and possibilities agreed upon by many astronomers and physicists, so I felt it important to expose my readers to some of these ideas. They do seem pretty dramatic and make for good reading particularly as it relates to how spectacular God can be when He is creating something from nothing. But the only thing we can be absolutely sure of is that "In the beginning God created the heavens and the earth." And that creation was indeed spectacular.

That being said, I think it is important to note here that while the Bible credits God for creating the universe in 6 days, those days were not the same six, 24-hour days as measured in today's world. Those first 6 days in Genesis were from God's perspective, not the human perspective living on earth billions of years later. This planet did not exist during the early universe so it would have been impossible to make a comparison between time in the early universe and time on our planet as measured today. We know that according to Einstein's law of relativity time is not static but flexible and is based on gravity and speed which caused time to be radically different during the early universe. We mentioned the time clock of the universe in an earlier chapter and will look at the flexibility of that time in the next chapter.

At the big bang, our entire visible universe was packed into a minuscule speck of space. Since then, expansion of the universe and the stretching of space has moved the "edge" of the universe out by billions of light years. Considering that each light year (the distance light travels in one year) is ten million million kilometers, it is clear that we live in a huge universe.

The big bang model of the early universe is extraordinarily simple: it has no structure of any kind on scales larger than individual elementary particles. Even though the behavior it predicts is governed only by general relativity, the Standard Model of elementary particle physics and the energy distribution rules of basic thermodynamics, it appears to describe the primordial fireball almost perfectly.

According to Jewish Orthodox physicist Gerald Schroeder, at the very beginning of the creation God, from nothing, put together a tiny amount of extremely high energy from dense hydrogen and helium which He created. This combination caused an immediate and instantaneous explosion which was the beginning of our universe. Scientists estimate that within 1/100th of second the circumference of the universe was about 4 light years across. Scientists of astronomy have been working to determine more precisely how the Big Bang unfolded and, in this chapter, I have used information from Steven Weinberg's book The First Three Minutes to expand on this subject.

The following paragraphs offer an unusual frame by frame look at microsecond views of the universe as it was unfolding. All of this can be found in Steven Weinberg's book The First Three Minutes. However, I have pared down the information, selecting those descriptions that are most understandable in order not to overwhelm readers. So here I have given only the highlights of those first 3 minutes. If you desire furthermore technical information, please read his book. Because each of these segments represent very short times Weinberg has used a camera and film to describe the sequence so that each view is called a frame as it would have been viewed should there have been someone capable of filming the sequence.

The discovery of the cosmic background Radiation (CBR), was first measured in 1941 by McKeller, and further observed and reported in 1965 by Penzias and Wilson. From this discovery a new understanding of the early universe has occurred, allowing astronomers, and physicists to develop a more accurate standard model of the first few minutes of the Big Bang. In the following paragraphs I have summarized some of this data for the first 3 minutes from the 1979 Nobel Prize book by Steven Weinberger.

While there is a bit of science to it, I think most readers will find it of interest even if only to better understand the magnitude of the explosion caused by the Big Bang. It really was quite amazing!

In his book The First Three Minutes Weinberg uses the idea of a camera snapping pictures at various moments in the explosion that followed the Big Bang. 119 Following the course of events through the first three minutes after the Big Bang. As time goes on, the time between recorded events increases. action slows so the first events are spaced much closer than later events, as the three minutes evolve the time between frames increases. In his book Weinberg adjusts the amount of time between frames to mimic the falling temperature of the universe, stopping the camera to take a picture each time that the temperature drops by a factor of about three.

Weinberg was unable to start the time at zero because there was no way of accurately knowing or describing the tiny spot of unimaginably hot and intense energy which would become our universe. So, the film starts about 100th of a second after the beginning explosion when the temperature had cooled to a mere one hundred thousand million degrees.

First Frame (approximately 1/100 of a second has passed)

The universe is so dense that even the neutrinos, which can travel for years through lead bricks without being scattered, are kept in thermal equilibrium with the electrons, positrons, and photons by rapid collisions with them and with each other. At this point, the universe is rapidly expanding at a rate just at escape velocity away from the center and cooling at a corresponding speed. Interestingly, because of the effect of gravity on time dilation, the age of the universe is actually less than the elapsed time of expansion. As mentioned earlier both gravity and speed influence time. In this case the universe was expanding faster than the clock, in essence if there had been a clock it would have been moving backwards. Therefore, the expansion of the universe would be less than the elapsed time of a clock. It's possible that the universe was about four light years in circumference. Since Light currently travels at about 186,000 miles per second, so in $1/100^{th}$ of a second, light could travel only 1,860 miles, but four light years would be 23.2 trillion miles, so how is that possible? Scientists that study the origin and development of the universe say the early universe was opaque so light could not travel through it as easily, and second, they theorize that the early universe went through a specific phase of expansion during which it grew at a rate faster than the speed of light.

Exceeding the speed of light would most likely be only possible in the early stages of the Big Bang because of the conditions. According to Kristine Spekkens (astronomer), There is a subtle difference between expansion that is faster than the speed of light and the propagation of information that is faster than the speed of light. The latter is forbidden by fundamental physical laws, but the former is allowed; that is, as long as you are not transmitting any information (like a light pulse), you can make something happen at a speed that is faster than that of light. The expansion of the Universe is a 'growth' of the spacetime itself; this spacetime may move faster than the speed of light relative to some other location, as long as the locations can't communicate with each other (or, in terms of light rays, these two parts of the Universe can't see each other). According to the theory of inflation, the Universe grew by a factor of 10 to the 60th power in less than 10 to the negative 30 seconds, so the 'edges' of the Universe were expanding away from each other faster than the speed of light; however, as long as those edges can't see each other (which is what we always assume), there is no physical law that forbids it.

In the previous paragraphs on early expansion of the universe, the key to understanding it lies in the last few sentences. The universe can expand faster than the speed of light as long the edges cannot see each other and there is no communication such as light (which can only travel at the speed of light) going on, which obviously there was not. Otherwise, it would not have been possible that the universe could expand faster than the speed of light. This is an interesting theoretical phenomenon.

Second Frame (.11 seconds have elapsed since the first frame)

According to Weinberg, at the next point, approximately .11 seconds after the previous point in time, the universe cooled to a mere 30,000 million degrees Kelvin. Little has changed in the makeup of the universe except that the nuclear particle balance has consequently shifted to 38 percent neutrons and 62 percent protons due to the reduced temperature. Time dilation has caused the elapsed time to increase to .2 seconds rather than .11 seconds. The total energy of the universe is about 30 million times denser than water at this point.

Third Frame (1.02 seconds have elapsed from the first frame)

At 1.09 seconds from the first discussed point, the mean temperature of the universe drops to 10,000 million degrees Kelvin. From now on the energy of the neutrinos and anti-neutrinos provides part of the gravitational field of the universe. At this time, the total energy is about 380,000 times denser than water. The characteristic time for expansion of the universe has correspondingly increased to about two seconds. The temperature is now only twice the threshold temperature of electrons and positrons, so they are just beginning to annihilate more rapidly than they can be recreated out of radiation.

Fourth Frame (13.82 seconds have elapsed since the first frame)

The temperature of the universe is now below the threshold temperature for electrons and positrons, so they are rapidly disappearing as major participants in the universe, and the energy released in their annihilation has slowed down the rate at which the universe cools.... It is now cool enough for various stable nuclei like helium (He^4) to form, but this does not happen immediately.... Neutrons are still being converted into protons, although much more slowly than before, the balance now is 17 percent neutrons and 83 percent protons.

Fifth Frame (three minutes and two seconds have elapsed)

"The temperature of the universe is now 1,000 million degrees Kelvin.... The electrons and positrons have mostly disappeared, and the chief constituents of the universe are now photons, neutrinos, and antineutrinos.... The neutrino-proton balance is now 14 percent neutrons, and 86 percent protons."

We will leave this method of presenting the first few minutes of the universe and trust that God not only knew exactly what He was doing, but was fully capable of bringing an amazing universe into being which would eventually create a planet earth capable of bringing forth life abundantly for all of His creatures.

God Always Begins at the Beginning

So, why would I have included all of this mind baffling information in a book about how God created the universe as compared to science. God always begins at the beginning; He never has to experiment or guess at how to do this. Before he began His creation of our universe, He knew exactly what He wanted to do, and how to go about it. The bible tells us very briefly how this came about but looking at science we get a much more detailed picture; and I think it is a good thing to know that God is in the details. Not only in our own personal lives but in everything He does. And He is never in a hurry.

All of science attests that: Nothing comes into existence partially done; this is a fact we take for granted. Prior to the big bang, God created wisdom, which contained the blueprint for the process of life in the universe. Science is still unable to determine exactly how it all began but agrees that there was a lot of energy in the form of light, which comes in discreet packets of photons. When photons are present with an abundance of energy, they spontaneously decay into elementary particles and antiparticles. All of these elementary particles and antiparticles were the building blocks of the universe.

As new measuring devices and more sophisticated telescopes are built, scientists can get closer to the big bang and actually see what it looked like. The closer they get to the origin of the universe, the more certain they become that there was a starting point, but even with this knowledge they are unable to go back past that point, and probably never will because before the universe was created, time, space, matter, and gravity did not exist, so there is nothing science can study.[22]

In this chapter I have tried to give enough detailed scientific information to give you a taste of how great our God is without completely overwhelming you. My sincere hope is that this chapter has highlighted not only the effort God made to build a home for us, but also the spectacular way in which He did that. He is our very spectacular God!

CHAPTER 9

A Different Frame of Reference

Time Dilation - a Different Frame of Reference

According to Wikipedia, Time dilation is a difference in the elapsed time measured by two clocks, either due to them having a velocity relative to each other, or by there being a gravitational potential difference between their locations.

To further explain the nature of time dilation we must understand a basic phenomenon of the law of relativity: the ticking of a clock at a location with high gravity or velocity is slower than the ticking of a clock at a location with lower gravity or velocity. According to Albert Einstein's law of relativity, travel speed, gravity, and time work together to establish a time continuum where events that occur at the same time for one observer could occur at different times for another. From that law astronomers determined that clocks could differ when they are moving through space at different speeds and exert a different gravitational force. This was certainly applicable to the newly expanding universe where matter was first being generated.

In this chapter we will gain a perspective on how time is affected by velocity, gravity, and speed. This information is the groundwork for understanding how time is relative to where it is being measured, and what I think is a plausible scientific explanation of how time changed between Genesis 1:1 and the sixth day of creation.

Gaining a Perspective

In a sandlot football game, both teams line up at scrimmage. The offensive team runs a play around their left end, but to the defensive team the player ran to the right. Who is right? Both are right but each side views what happed from their own perspective. Similarly, one who reads the first three chapters in the book of Genesis must see the creation of the universe not from their perspective but from God's perspective. He is the author, and His perspective is obviously going to be different from our human perspective billions of years after the universe began because time has changed throughout the millennium of the existence of the universe. Time as we measure it today on this planet is still changing and was not the same as time when God began creating the universe. The problem is that we as humans assume time is going to be exactly the same everywhere just as it is here today on our tiny planet. But it isn't, time is relative to when, and where it is being measured.

Time itself is different for observers in different frames of reference, when one frame is in motion relative to another or in a different place. At lower speeds, the difference is imperceptible, but as the moving frame of reference approaches the speed of light, the difference becomes more noticeable. Gravity also has an impact on the perceived speed, or clock, so that a strong gravitational force will exert more change on time than another location with a weaker gravity.

Scientists used to look at the stars and see that they were always there, steady state. They had always been there and always would be there. And Humankind has always had some concept of time. It is the cycle of light and dark, the change in the season, the ticking of the clock. Time was a constant that had nothing to do with anything else. Then along came Albert Einstein, who theorized that in the physical sciences nothing is absolute, everything is relative to everything else, even time. Time is relative to speed and depends on the relation of the observer and the observed.

An Example of How Time Dilation Works

Imagine you have a twin. Your twin boards a spaceship and flies to some far away star at nearly the speed of light. You stay here on Earth. For your twin, the trip takes about a year, but when he returns to Earth, you have aged nearly twenty years. For your twin, traveling at nearly the speed of light, time actually passes much more slowly than it does for you here on Earth. Less actual time elapsed for your twin because they were traveling at nearly the speed of light. For you, the object at rest, time passed at the normal speed. Because time is relative to speed, as speed increases to nearly the speed of light, time actually slows. This phenomenon was actually proven in 1919 by Arthur Stanley Eddington's according to the Wikipedia article, The History of General Relativity.

Einstein's theory of relativity indicates that for a vehicle traveling at the speed or velocity of light, no time elapses, so a clock in the vehicle registers no change. To take this a step further, Astronomer Kristin Spekkens, science director for the Square Kilometer Array, and professor at the Royal Military College of Canada and Queen's University, speculates that in the early expansion of the universe, in specific situations, matter actually exceeded the speed of light, and had there been a clock it would have been going backwards.

An Imaginary Trip Through Time

Imagine you are on the bridge of the Starship Enterprise, exploring a massive black hole that was once the center of our galaxy, the Milky Way. The black hole was once a star estimated to have been 2.5 million times larger than our own sun. When that star collapsed to a singularity all of its matter condensed into a spot in space with infinite density the size of a grain of sand. The gravitational power it exerted was so intense that nothing, not even light itself, could escape.

The commander of your starship sends one of its exploratory ships to inspect the black hole. As the ship approaches the edge of the black hole, the commander notices that the craft begins to slow down, and in fact, seems to have stopped moving.

On the exploratory craft, everything seems normal. The captain of the exploratory ship collects the necessary data about the singularity on the ship's computer and prepares to navigate back to the Enterprise. However, as they approach the coordinates where they left the Enterprise, they find nothing but empty space. A passing starship provides a startling revelation: While a mere hour had passed on the exploratory ship, thousands of years had passed outside the singularity. This is the effect of intense gravity on time.

Time Dilation and Genesis

This brings us back to Genesis and the discrepancy between six days and fifteen billion years. So, let us look at the frames of reference in these two times. God provides the perspective for Genesis, and His frame of reference is the entire universe, not a singular point in it. So, the question is, how did time unfold in this cosmic frame of reference and how was it recorded. To understand how

God sees time and records it, we must define God's clock. A clock is anything that repeats itself periodically such that the rhythm of its repeating cycles can be used to note the passage of time. A clock does not create time; it merely records it.

God does not actually need a clock because He sees all that ever was, all that is now, and ever will be all at the same time. That being said, in order to communicate His creation to humankind, He would become a part of the world He was creating, and at the same time create a paradigm that we as humans could understand. He chose to use a clock of the whole universe and express that in 24-hour days. Not our 24-hour days, but His 24-hour days. This enabled us to possess a record of His creation for all time. God's Genesis clock measured days based on His clock of the whole universe, and He left a remnant of that clock, CBR, as a record for us at some point in history, to determine and understand what those 24-hour days were. Then He recorded those 6 days in the book of Genesis.

So, how does this work?

In Chapter 7, under time of the universe, we discussed how light was used to develop the clock of the universe, and then in the previous paragraphs in this chapter, using CBR as a consistent remnant of light from the early universe we were able to measure the passage of time during that unfolding of the universe.

But what exactly is CBR or CMBR

According to Scientific American Magazine, Cosmic Background Radiation, (or as it is now called, *Cosmic Microwave Background radiation* or CMB), is a faint glow of light that fills the universe, falling on Earth from every direction with nearly uniform intensity. This light set out on its journey billions of years ago, long before the Earth or even our galaxy existed. In Chapter I,

BACKSTAGE WITH GOD

A journey, we briefly explained that CBR or Cosmic Background Radiation was discovered by two Astronomers, Arno Penzias and Robert Wilson in 1965 and "is the only source of radiation that has been present and ubiquitous since the creation." In order to compare time today with time at the big bang, we need to understand that CBR is a valid indicator of the speed of the clock during the early expansion of the universe because it actually existed at the time of the big bang and still exists today exactly as it was at the time of the Big Bang. According to Gerald Schroeder "CBR fills the entire universe unrelated to any particular source. . . (and). . . is the only source of radiation that has been present and unchanged since the creation" CBR is measured in cycles per second (or Hertz), and is also called frequency.

The following is a greatly simplified version of how CBR and the cosmic clock worked:

- There is a direct relationship between the stretching of space and CBR: As the universe stretched at the instant of the big bang, the frequency of the CBR decreased.
- The decrease in CBR frequency caused the wavelength of the CBR to stretch. As the frequency decreased the wavelength (the length of a cycle) stretched out or increased
- This increase in the wavelength caused the cosmic clock used in Genesis to slow way down.
- According to Dr. Schroeder at the time of the big bang, the ratio between today's clock and the cosmic clock was a million million to one. Put another way, the cosmic clock at the time of the big bang was running approximately a trillion times slower than today's clock.
- As the universe doubled during each of the Genesis "days," it took longer to expand the universe. Therefore, day two covered half as many current years as day 1 and each day thereafter covered half as many current years as the previous day.

- The Genesis clock started with the creation of the universe and continued until the creation of humankind. After the earth was formed, towards the end of day six when Adam came on the scene, some billions of current-clock years after the Big Bang, the two clocks—the cosmic clock came into sync with the earth clock. And the life of Adam and those following him were recorded as actual earth years in Genesis.
- This briefly explains how the 15.75 billion years of universe-building reckoned by science fit into the six days of creation discussed in Genesis. I will further illustrate this point in another section of this book.

The original frequency of the CBR was approximately 3 cycles per second. (or 3 hertz) As the universe expanded, this frequency slowly increased, decreasing the wavelength and speeding up the cosmic clock until it synced with our current clock towards the end of day six, when Adam appeared and the length of lifetimes began recording as years in Genesis. However, the original frequency of CBR from the Big Bang still exists unchanged as it was recorded in 1965, and today still registers the actual clock speed at the time of the creation. Whereas the clock of Genesis was operating at a much slower rate than today's earth clock, those 6 days in Genesis match up with the Billions of earth years claimed by scientists for the entire existence of the universe.

In Review

When scientists discuss the age of the universe as being 13 or 14 or 15 billion years what does that actually mean? It means that they are stating time based on equivalent earth years which is not necessarily relevant to any other place or time in the universe. Elapsed time on a clock is never static, i.e., a year on earth is not necessarily the same as a year on any other place or time in the universe. When looking at the whole universe, time is based on gravity and speed of travel, and those two dimensions differ throughout the universe. Time in the universe is very dynamic, not static as it might be in one place or time.

The only relevant measurement that will connect an earth time clock to a clock of the universe running at a different speed is that small remnant of light scientists call **CBR** or cosmic background radiation. The speed of the early clock of the universe is based on the CBR frequency from the Big Bang, which is 3 cycles per second.

Scientists ignore the differences between the elapsed speeds of these two clocks because there is no way to intelligently relate an earlier much slower elapsed time to our current elapsed time for the purpose of communication. But those billions of years would only be relevant to us today on planet earth and would not be relevant to someone if they were living during the early universe. If they had both their universe clock and an earth clock ticking alongside each other, their clock would seem to be advancing in a normal rate, while an earth clock would be a blur of speed recording time in billions of years. Just as an astronaut traveling at near the speed of light would register normal elapsed time, the same clock on earth would be ticking at a much faster rate, registering years.

To gain an understanding, and a rational mental comparison between the elapsed time of two clocks running at different speeds it would be necessary to accept one clock or the other as the standard of measurement. Science has chosen the earth clock as the standard by which they measure the age of the universe. That was their choice to make, however God chose to use the clock of the universe as His standard when He wrote Genesis, and I think that was the logical choice since there was no earth for many of those years. So, when scientists say that the universe is so many billions of years old, those are equivalent earth years, but not the actual number of years if you were living in the early universe. If one could project an earth clock against the clock of the early universe the two would not match up. While the earth clock would be registering billions of years, the clock of the universe would be registering 24-hour days. Similarly, an astronaut traveling at near the speed of light would register very little elapsed time while on earth the clocks would be ticking at their regular speed, registering hours, days, and years.

All of this comes down to one's perspective. Looking from planet earth backwards to the Big Bang we measure elapsed time with our earth clocks in billions of years. But from the perspective of the new universe where time would seem perfectly normal, that same earth clock would be registering billions of years. So, when we read Genesis and the 6 days of creation, we have to change our perspective and forget earth days or years. Because God wrote the book of Genesis, we need to have His perspective, and that perspective is much slower than an equivalent earth clock today. In the next chapter we make a comparison between the two clocks days to years.

CHAPTER 10

Harmony Between Modern Science and The Bible

A Comparison

The days/years of our universe according to the bible and science

In this chapter we will break the passage of time down into the 6 days as recorded in the book of Genesis, i.e., God's time in the development of the Universe. Then we will compare the same time with what science said for that same time

DAY 1 lasted 8 billion years according to science, but according to Genesis it was Day 1 Gen. 1: 1- 5 "In the beginning God created the heavens and the earth. 2- The earth was without form and void, and darkness was on the face of the deep. And the Spirit of God was hovering over the face of the waters. 3-Then God said, 'let there be light; and there was light,' 4- And God saw the light, that it was good, and God divided the light from the darkness. 5-God called the light Day and the darkness He called Night. So, the evening and the morning were the first day."

In the Bible: The creation of the universe; light separates from darkness. Note: There is no word in either Hebrew or Aramaic for universe. In the NT the word is Cosmos for universe. The waters are really representing everything there was and, Darkness is the symbol for chaos.

According to science: This period of time was from 15.75 billion years ago to 7.75 billion years ago. Immediately following the big bang, in a miniscule fraction of a second the universe expanded from its point at creation to a size similar to that of our solar system, and according to Weinberg, as noted in the 7th chapter of this book, at .0008 seconds the universe would be about 4 light years across, or 24 trillion miles from one side to the other side. Expansion allowed the universe to expand faster than the speed of light for a short period of time. At the instant of the big bang everything sub-atomic, the elemental particles that would constitute today's world, the quarks, protons, neutrons, electrons as well as time, space, gravity and all of the laws of nature and quantum mechanics were included in that small spot of energy. All of this would become stardust later and make up the stars, galaxies, and planets we see today. Light literally breaks free as electrons bond to atomic nuclei; galaxies start to form. However, initially the intensity of energy and heat was so incredibly high no light could escape. It was actually the first black hole. Initially there was no light at all, only a swirling opaque ball of mass energy. It was only at a point when this primordial mass had cooled, and gravitational forces were reduced enough to permit electromagnetic radiation to escape that light could have been seen. So, let there be light, (which would have been visible), was a separate event from the initial creation of light in both the bible and science. During the early period of that 8 billion years the stars and galaxies began forming.

DAY 2 Lasted 4 billion years according to science, from 7.75 to 3.75 billion years ago. Day 2 Gods time Gen. 1:6-8 "Then God said, 'let there be a firmament in the midst of the waters and let it divide the waters from the waters.' 7-Thus God made the firmament and divided the waters which were under the firmament from the waters that were above the firmament, and it was so. And God called the firmament heaven. So, the evening and the morning were the second day."

According to the Bible: The heavenly firmament forms.

According to science: The heavens as we know them were created. The chaos that would eventually be known as earth was separated from the rest of creation, and our own galaxy, the Milky Way formed as did our sun and earth in its earliest formation. According to science the sun, a main sequence star located in the spiral, formed 4.6 billion years ago. The oldest stars of the Milky Way are found in globular clusters, outside the spiral disk, and are barely visible to unaided vision.

DAY 3 Lasted 2 billion years according to science from 3.75 to 1.75 billion years ago. Day 3 God's time Gen. 1:9-13 "Then God said, 'let the waters under the heaven's be gathered together into one place, and let the dry land appear;' and it was so. 2-And God called the dry land Earth, and the gathering together of waters He called seas. And God saw that it was good. 11-Then God said, 'Let the earth bring forth grass, the herb that yields seed, and the fruit tree that yields fruit according to its kind, whose seed is in itself, on the earth;' and it was so. 12- And the earth brought forth grass, and herb that yields seed according to its kind, and the tree that yields fruit, whose seed is in itself according to its kind. And God saw that it was good. 13-So the evening and the morning were the third day."

According to the Bible: Oceans and dry land appear; the first life, plants appear (Gen. 1:9-13); the kabbalah states this marked only the start of plant life, which then developed during the following days.

According to science: "From geophysical evidence of weathered rocks, we learn that Earth had cooled, and liquid water appeared on it 3.8 billion years ago, and fossil data have demonstrated that the first simple plant life appeared immediately after liquid water and not billions of years later."

However, the kabbalah teaches that there was no particular day this happened but rather over the 2 billion years of day 3. The oceans and the dry land appeared as well as the first plant life. The earth cooled, liquid water formed and almost immediately the first life appears, plant and animal life photosynthesis, bacteria, algae and bacteria appeared.

DAY 4 Lasted 1 billion years according to science from 1.75 to 750 million years ago. Day 4 God's time Gen. 1:14-19 14- "Then God said, 'let there be lights in the firmament of the heavens to divide the day from the night; and let them be for signs and seasons, and for days and years. 15-And let them be for lights in the firmament of the heavens to give light on the earth.' And it was so. 16-Then God made two great lights: the greater light to rule the day, and the lesser light to rule the night. He made the stars also. 17-God set them in the firmament of the heavens to give light on the earth, and 18-to rule over the day and over the night, and to divide the light from the darkness. And God saw that it was good. 19- So the evening and the morning were the 4th day."

According to the Bible: The Sun, Moon, and stars became visible in the heavens.

According to science: Initially the atmosphere had been nearly opaque then with the rising concentrations of oxygen the atmosphere would have become translucent and the sun moon and stars would have appeared from the surface of the earth.

DAY 5 Lasted 500 million years according to science from 750 million years to 250 million years ago

Day 5 God's time Gen. 1:20-23 "Then God said, 'let the waters abound with an abundance of living creatures, and let birds fly above the earth across the face of the firmament of the heavens.' 21-So God created great sea creatures and every living thing that moves, with which the waters abounded, according to their kind, and every winged bird according to its kind. And God saw that it was good. 22-And God blessed them, saying 'be fruitful and multiply, and fill the waters in the seas, and let birds multiply on the earth.' 23-So the evening and the morning were the fifth day."

According to Science: First multicellular animals; waters swarm with animal life having the basic body plans of all future animals; winged insects appear. Life is created in the oceans and the first reptiles and birds appear, initially sea life would have been dominant, and then came the Cambrian era. An explosion of life occurred about 530 million years ago when every species of land animal literally appeared at the same time. Fossil records bear this out, and then about 360 million years ago in rapid succession amphibian reptiles and winged insect life appeared.

DAY 6 Lasted 250 million years according to science from 250 million years to Adam when biblical time began being recorded. Day 6 God's Time Gen. 1:24-31 Then God said, 24- "'let the earth bring forth the living creature according to its kind; cattle and creeping thing and beast of the earth, each according to its kind;' and it was so. 25-And God made the beast of the earth according to its kind, cattle according to its kind, and everything that creeps on the earth according to its kind. And God saw that it was good. 26-Then God said, 'let us make man in our image, according to our likeness; let them have dominion over the fish of the sea, over the birds of the air and over the cattle, over all the earth over every creeping thing that creeps on the earth.' 27-So God created man in His own image; in the image of God He created him; male and female He created them. 28-Then God blessed them, and God said to them, be fruitful and multiply; fill the earth and subdue it; have dominion over the fish of the sea, over the birds of the air and over every living thing that moves on the earth. 29-And God said,' see I have given you every herb that yields seed which is on the face of all the earth, and every tree whose fruit yields seed; to you it shall be for food. 30-Also, to every beast of the earth to every bird of the air, and to everything that creeps on the earth. In which there is life, I have given every green herb for food;' and it was so. 31-Then God saw everything that He had made, and indeed it was very good. So, the evening and the morning were the sixth day."

According to the Bible: Land animals, mammals; humankind created.

According to science: 250 million years ago, there was a mass extinction of 90% of all life on earth followed by a rapid repopulation of land animals, mammals predominating (the Permian-Triassic era) There have been 5 to 20 extinction events on earth. About 250 million years ago the dinosaurs appeared and dominated life on earth for about 150 million years. Then 65 million years ago another extinction known as the KT extinction killed off the dinosaurs and opened the way for mammals and birds to become the dominant life. Then the first hominids and finally human beings appeared. From the moment God breathed His Nefesh into man and gave him his soul the earth has noted the passage of time by clocks. Even while time is slowing down it is not noticeable today because it happens so slowly. And thus ends Backstage with God.

Some of the descriptions with regard to what science says in chapter 10 are from discussions in the movie The Genesis Code as well as from the books of Gerald L. Schroeder which were almost identical.

This ending may still leave questions in your head about "mankind" and it does with me also. Were there two separate creations of mankind in day six of Genesis, i.e., Ch. 1 vs 26 and Ch 2 vs 7?

This isn't the end of that discussion. In my next book I will tackle my thoughts on that subject as well as others such as Darwin's theory of evolution vs the clockmaker's version, an intelligent design to first life.

We may not have all the answers as to how this story begins, but we know how it ends!

To God be the Glory. I will sing forever of His goodness!

BIBLIOGRAPHY

Craig, William Lane, *A Reasonable Response*: Answers to Tough Questions on God, Christianity and the Bible, (Chicago: Moody Press, 2013)

Nahamanides, *commentary on Genesis*, Talmud Hagigah 12A,

Schroeder, Gerald L. *Genesis and the Big Bang: The discovery Of Harmony Between Modern Science and The Bible*. New York: Bantam Books, 1990.

———. *God According to God: A Scientist Discovers We've Been Wrong About God All Along*. New York: Harper Collins, 2009.

———. *The Hidden Face of God: Science Reveals the Ultimate Truth*. New York: Simon and Schuster, 2001.

———. *The Science of God: The Convergence of Scientific and Biblical Wisdom*. New York: The Free Press, Simon & Schuster, 1997.

Spekkens, Kristine - Ph.D. Cornell 2005 *Ask an Astronomer* –

Wald, George. "*The Origins of Life*." Scientific American, August 1954.

Weinberg, Steven. *The First Three Minutes: A Modern Version of the Origin of The Universe*. New York:BasicBooks A Division of HarperCollins, 1988

———. *Life in the Universe, Scientific American* 1995

REFERENCES

1 - Gerald L. Schroeder, The Science of God: The Convergence of Scientific and Biblical Wisdom. New York: The Free Press, Simon & Schuster, (186) Manuscript (7 6)

2 -Andy Stanley. Pastor North Point Community Church, Alpharetta, Georgia: (8 6)

3 -William Lane Craig. A Reasonable Response. Answers to Tough Questions on God, Christianity and the Bible. Chicago: Moody Press, 2013. 212

4-William Lane Craig. A Reasonable Response. Answers to Tough Questions on God, Christianity and the Bible. Chicago: Moody Press, 2013. 212

5 -Phillips, Craig, and Dean's song, your grace still amazes me, your love still a mystery.

6-Author's Thoughts

7- Gerald L. Schroeder, The Science of God: The Convergence of Scientific and Biblical Wisdom. New York: The Free Press, Simon & Schuster, 186

8-Gerald L. Schroeder, God According to God: A Scientist Discovers We've Been Wrong About God All Along. New York: Harper Collins, 2009. 51

9-Gerald L. Schroeder, The Science of God, The Convergence of Scientific and Biblical Wisdom. New York: The Free Press, Simon & Schuster, 1997, 17

[10] - Gerald L. Schroeder, The Hidden Face of God: New York: The Free Press, Simon & Schuster, 1997, 4

[11] - Gerald L. Schroeder, The Science of God: The Convergence of Scientific and Biblical Wisdom. New York: The Free Press, Simon & Schuster, 1997, 171

[12] -Gerald L. Schroeder, The Hidden Face of God: New York: The Free Press, Simon & Schuster, 1997, 212

[13] -Gerald L. Schroeder, God according to God, A Scientist Discovers We've Been Wrong About God All Along. New York: Harper Collins, 2009. 103

[14] -Gerald L. Schroeder. The Hidden Face of God: New York: The Free Press, Simon & Schuster, 1997, 4

[15] -Gerald L. Schroeder. The Hidden Face of God: New York: The Free Press, Simon & Schuster, 1997, 40

[16] - Gerald L. Schroeder, God According to God: A Scientist Discovers We've Been Wrong About God All Along. New York: Harper Collins, 2009. 130

[17] Gerald L. Schroeder. Genesis and the Big Bang: The discovery Of Harmony Between Modern Science and The Bible. New York: Bantam Books, 1990. 88-89

[18] - Gerald L. Schroeder, The Science of God, The Convergence of Scientific and Biblical Wisdom. New York: The Free Press, Simon & Schuster, 1997, 21

[19] -William Lane Craig. A Reasonable Response. Answers to Tough Questions on God, Christianity and the Bible. Chicago: Moody Press, 2013.

[20] -Gerald L. Schroeder, The Science of God, The Convergence of Scientific and Biblical Wisdom. New York: The Free Press, Simon & Schuster, 1997, 149-152

[21] -Gerald L. Schroeder. Genesis and the Big Bang: The discovery Of Harmony Between Modern Science and The Bible. New York: Bantam Books, 1990, 156

[22]-Weinberg, Steven. *The First Three Minutes: A Modern Version of the Origin of The Universe.* New York: Basic Books A Division of HarperCollins, 1988